Free in the Sea

Lynne Cox's Story

By Michael Sandler

Scott Foresman
is an imprint of

Glenview, Illinois • Boston, Massachusetts • Chandler, Arizona •
Upper Saddle River, New Jersey

Illustrations
8, 12, 16 Jeff Grunewald.

Photographs

Every effort has been made to secure permission and provide appropriate credit for photographic material. The publisher deeply regrets any omission and pledges to correct errors called to its attention in subsequent editions.

Unless otherwise acknowledged, all photographs are the property of Pearson Education, Inc.

Photo locators denoted as follows: Top (T), Center (C), Bottom (B), Left (L), Right (R), Background (Bkgd)

Opener Patrik Giardino/Corbis; **1** Corbis; **4** Patrik Giardino/Corbis; **7** Eric Schweikardt/ Getty Images; **10** ©National Geographic/SuperStock; **14** Getty Images; **18** Ralph A Clevenger/PhotoLibrary Group, Inc.; **19** Corbis; **20** ©Epoque/Pictorial Parade/Getty Images; **21** Patrik Giardino/Corbis; **22** (BR) Fritz Prenzel/Peter Arnold, Inc., (BL) Mark Boulton/Alamy Images, (TL) Photos to Go/Photolibrary, (TR) Vince Streano/Corbis.

ISBN 13: 978-0-328-51433-5
ISBN 10:   0-328-51433-0

7 8 9 10 V0FL 16 15 14 13

Table of Contents

Lynne Cox sat on the steps of the boat. Her feet dangled inches above the freezing Antarctic water. The water was cold enough to kill a person in minutes. And Lynne was about to jump in—wearing nothing but a swimsuit and goggles. Lynne was afraid, but she reminded herself that this was her choice. She wanted to be free. She wanted to see what she could do. She wanted to break down the borders of the impossible.

Learning to Swim

From the day she was born, Lynne Cox was meant to be a swimmer. As a baby, her parents taught her how to swim in the bathtub. They taught her how to move her arms, kick her legs, and blow bubbles in the water. Baby Lynne would swim right across the bathtub. For her, swimming came as naturally as walking. By the time Lynne was three years old, she was practicing her strokes in chilly Snow Lake.

Snow Lake, located in Maine, is where her family spent their summer vacations.

Lynne and her siblings, David, Laura, and Ruth, grew up in New Hampshire. They were all very skilled swimmers. However, of the four children, Lynne loved being in the water the most. When other children on Lynne's grade school swim team grew tired and begged to leave the pool, nine-year-old Lynne did the opposite. She pleaded with the coach: *Let me stay in!* In fact, Lynne enjoyed the water the most when her teammates got out. That's when she felt free, when no other swimmers crowded around her.

On one cold and gusty day, the weather drove Lynne's teammates inside. Lynne decided to stay in the pool with a group of college swimmers. The wind started to whip up the water and large raindrops began to fall. When the rain increased, even the college swimmers decided to get out of the water. But nothing would discourage Lynne. She kept swimming, enjoying the strangely shimmering water and the sweet taste of raindrops on her lips. Later she wrote, "...by putting myself in a situation different from everyone else's, I had experienced something different, beautiful, and amazing."

Moving to California

Lynne was twelve when her family moved to California. The primary reason for the move was to find better swim training for the children. There were not many good coaches near their home in New Hampshire. They found Lynne's new coach, Don Gambril, in California. He had trained some of the world's best swimmers. These athletes included Olympic swimmers Mark Spitz and Sharon Stouder.

Lynne trained with Gambril for more than two years. After working with him for awhile, she began to get frustrated. For some reason Lynne wasn't getting any faster. Something wasn't right. Gambril noticed that Lynne got stronger the longer she swam. Pool races were not long enough to make the most of her talent. He suggested that she start to race in the ocean instead. Ocean races were much longer than pool races. They could be up to three miles or longer.

Lynne's first ocean race was the Seal Beach Rough Water Swim. Lynne and the other racers stood on the beach waiting for the starting gun to sound. When it fired, the swimmers dove into the ocean surf. Right away, Lynne loved the difference. Here there were no walls, lanes, or limits, just beautiful open water. Lynne felt as though she were flying like a bird as she cut through the waves. This was very different from swimming in a pool. She felt she was "going from a cage to freedom." From now on, Lynne decided she would swim only in the ocean.

The Catalina Channel

In 1971, now fourteen years old, Lynne joined a group of teenage ocean swimmers with a special goal. They were planning a long distance swim across the Catalina **Channel**. The channel, some twenty miles wide, separates Catalina Island from the California **mainland**. No teen group had ever attempted to swim the channel before.

The team had been training for a year, but it was easy to see that Lynne was the fastest swimmer. No matter how each girl did individually, they all helped push one another to do their best. They knew that in order to complete their goal, they would need to train long and hard. They practiced at night, when the sea was nearly pitch-black. With their coach watching, the teenagers jumped into

Los Angeles

Seal Beach

CALIFORNIA

Catalina Channel

Catalina Island

Pacific Ocean

N
W   E
S

the water beneath the light of the moon. They swam for three or four hours at a time.

When the big day arrived, Lynne's team hopped aboard a fishing boat. They rode out to Catalina Island, spending most of the two-and-a-half hour trip below deck. The swimmers were afraid to look at the ocean before their swim. They believed that if they saw how far the journey was, they might be too frightened to go through with it.

At midnight, the swimmers began their crossing of the Catalina Channel. Lynne felt nervous and excited as she tore through the water. She told herself not to look back or think about sharks. However, her biggest concern was getting lost. The water was so dark that the swimmers couldn't see their own arms, let alone each other. A guide boat cruised in front of them to light the way, but its tiny lights were too dim. Even with lifeguards paddling next to them in kayaks, the swimmers felt isolated in the vast ocean.

Although they could have let their fears stop them, the five teenagers swam on and on. Stroke after stroke, mile after mile, they pressed on, keeping their goal in mind. Every hour or two they paused to have something to drink.

The members of the crew on the boat tossed the swimmers bottles of water and warm cider. Then **fatigue** set in. One swimmer quit, saying, "I'm cold. I can't go on." The other three had a difficult time keeping up with Lynne. She would swim ahead and then wait for them to catch up. Each time she waited, her body grew colder.

Then Lynne got some news from the crew who were keeping track of her time. If Lynne kept up her present **pace**, she would break the Catalina Channel speed record. This wasn't even a youth record; it was the world record for any swimmer, young or old, male or female.

The Catalina Channel

"Go for it," the crew shouted. Lynne's coach said she could do it—if she wanted to.

Lynne couldn't believe it. Treading water, she thought hard. "I want to do it so badly," she said, "but I can't." Lynne had started with the team and she was going to finish with the team. They had all worked too hard for Lynne to take the glory. The whole team deserved to reach their goal as a group. So she stayed with the others, helping guide them to shore after twelve and a half hours in the ocean.

The English Channel

Lynne felt proud that her team had reached their goal, but she also knew the truth. The team had held her back. She could have beaten a world record if she had been alone. Swimming by herself, she would be free to go as fast as her heart desired. From now on, Lynne decided she would swim alone.

For her next challenge, Lynne chose the English Channel. This body of water separates England from France. For long distance swimmers, crossing it is like climbing Mount Everest or playing in a Super Bowl. Although the English Channel is as wide as the Catalina Channel, crossing it is much more difficult. The biggest difference is water temperature. English Channel waters are much colder than the waters off southern California.

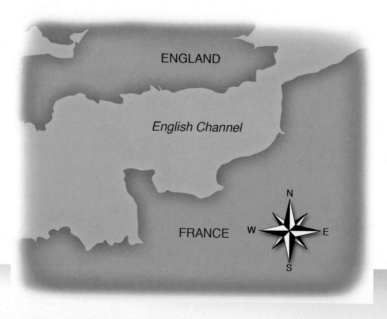

ENGLAND

English Channel

FRANCE

Lynne tried to prepare herself. When winter came, she refused to wear sweaters or jackets. She walked around in sandals instead of wearing socks and shoes. She trained early in the morning, before the sun warmed the ocean. Sometimes, gliding through the dark cold sea, Lynne imagined that she was traveling through outer space.

Even in training, Lynne continued to attend school. Her principal let her show up late, as long as she kept her grades high. After nearly a year of practice, Lynne flew to England with her mother in 1972. There she hired a boat **pilot** to guide and protect her on her swim. The pilot was surprised that the fifteen-year-old American girl wasn't planning simply a crossing. She was planning to set an English Channel speed record.

When Lynne dove into the Channel, she felt a surge of energy. "I didn't have to wait for anyone," she later wrote." I could swim at my own pace.…"

The pace she chose was blazingly fast. She only stopped for swigs of juice and to ask the pilot about the strange soft balls she felt bounce off her body. The balls turned out to be heads of lettuce dumped in the water by a ship.

As she neared the French coast, Lynne's arms grew tired. Worst of all, she was hungry. She dreamed of hamburgers and milkshakes. Instead, she settled for soggy, salty cookies tossed into the water by her mother. Fighting strong **currents**, Lynne pressed on against the pain. She pictured the faces of the people who believed in her. She could not quit and let them down. Finally, as her mother and the pilot shouted wildly from the boat, Lynne crashed through the waves onto the rocks of the French coast. She had done it! The swim had taken nine hours and fifty-seven minutes—a new world record, and 46 minutes faster than the old record!

Lynne Cox after her record breaking English Channel swim

The Bering Strait

Lynne went on to college and even more difficult swims. However, she became less interested in breaking records. Instead, she focused on testing the limits of her own **endurance**. She wanted to swim where people said it was impossible. To Lynne, this was what kept her free.

In 1975, she became the first woman in history to swim New Zealand's Cook Strait. In order to do so, she braved eight-foot waves and ferocious winds. A year later, at the tip of South America, Lynne crossed the Strait of Magellan. No other human being had swum this icy stretch where the Atlantic and Pacific Oceans meet violently. It was a dangerous journey. The merging of these oceans has been known to create whirlpools that can drag down ships.

And in 1987, after ten long years of planning, Lynne took on the Bering Strait. The Bering Strait is a body of water that separates Russia and the United States. At that time, when Russia was part of the Soviet Union (U.S.S.R.), the Bering Strait was the border between two **hostile** countries. The United States and the U.S.S.R. did not get along. They were involved in what is known as the Cold War. The Cold

War was a struggle between the two nations over everything from weapons to industry and technology. This conflict lasted for more than 40 years. During this time, each country threatened the other many times with nuclear missiles.

The closest point between the two countries lies between two tiny islands. Little Diomede, part of Alaska, is on the American side of the Bering Strait. Big Diomede, its larger but matching island, is on the Soviet side. The islands are only three miles apart, but at that time, the distance seemed like more than a thousand miles. For forty years, the water between the islands was closed. No person or ship had passed between them. In addition, the people on the island of Little Diomede could not visit relatives on Big Diomede. Between the weapons and the divided families, the situation between the United States and the U.S.S.R. was very difficult. By swimming between the islands, Lynne hoped to break down the wall that divided the two nations.

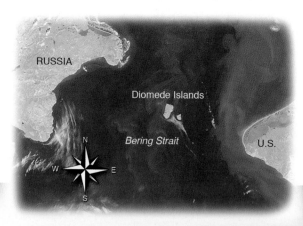

Before Lynne could plunge into her bravest crossing, she needed permission to swim ashore at Big Diomede. She got to work writing hundreds of letters and making thousands of phone calls to both Soviet and American officials. She contacted congressmen, senators, even presidents. Finally, after many attempts, she was able to get some important people on her side. With the help of senators, congressmen, and ambassadors, she got permission to come ashore on Big Diomede. Then Lynne spent every penny she had to put together a team for the crossing. For days before the swim, she ate only bagels and peanut butter, because she couldn't afford anything else. All of her money had gone for tickets to Alaska, helicopter and boat rental on Little Diomede, and the expenses for her team of doctors.

The doctors were a very important part of this journey. Though short, the Bering Strait swim would be her most dangerous crossing. No swimmer in the world had ever survived a crossing in waters as cold as these. The Bering Strait stayed frozen most of the year. The ice didn't melt until the middle of July. Even then, water temperatures were below 40 degrees. The people on Little Diomede Island didn't bother to learn how to swim. They knew in the frigid Bering Strait, a person would die within minutes from the cold water—if they weren't eaten first by a Great Pacific shark.

When Lynne finally jumped into the Bering Strait, the water felt like liquid ice. Still, the extreme coldness of the strait didn't seem to bother her. She felt strong, powerful, and energetic. Not too long into her journey, a thick, blinding fog came down upon the Channel. Her team worried they'd get lost and miss Big Diomede.

But Lynne was determined to reach her goal. She knew that this challenge was greater then being the first person to swim across the Bering Strait. It was about bringing people and countries together. With this in mind, she powered on through the frigid, shark-infested waters. She swam without anything to protect her. She even swam past walruses!

Then, a Soviet boat appeared in the darkness. Lynne had crossed the border! Her team celebrated the fact that Lynne had swum where

The waters of the Bering Strait off of Little Diomede Island are some of the roughest and coldest waters in the world.

no man had swum before. The Soviet pilot guided her and the crew onto the shore at Big Diomede.

Her body completely numb, Lynne stumbled out of the sea. The Soviets smiled and cheered, extending their hands to help her. They covered her frozen body in warm blankets. They treated her as if she were one of their own. She truly had connected with these people through her amazing feat.

A few months later, Soviet President Mikhail Gorbachev and American President Ronald Reagan met together at the White House. Their goal was to shrink the number of weapons each country had aimed at the other. Gorbachev held up his glass and spoke: *"Last summer it took one brave American by the name of Lynne Cox just two hours to swim from one of our countries to the other. ...She proved by her courage how close to each other our peoples live."*

Antarctica and Beyond

One might think that after all these amazing crossings Lynne would decide to retire. While that may happen someday, for now Lynne keeps looking for new challenges. In December 2002, she took on the planet's coldest continent. Wearing only a swimsuit, Lynne jumped from her seat on the steps of a boat into the ice-filled waters off Antarctica. Even for Lynne, this swim was extreme. The water temperature was 32 degrees, right at the freezing point.

Lynne said, "I really didn't know how long I could last or if I would be okay." Surprisingly, she was fine. At one point, she found herself swimming with a group of penguins. She said she considered this a good sign, since it meant there were no killer whales in the area. From start to finish, it took her about 25 minutes to swim to Antarctica's shore.

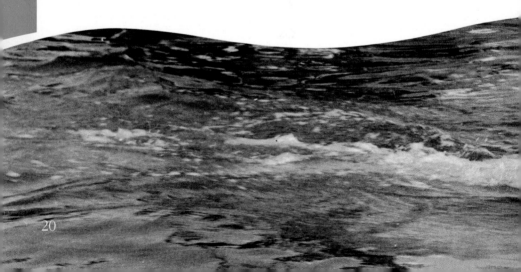

Lynne may never stop looking for places to test her limits, places to swim where no one else will try. If a challenge comes along, she will be up for it. To Lynne, swimming is all about freedom; freedom for herself and freedom for others.

Lynne often uses her swims as a way of connecting people and trying to bring about peace, just as she did with her swim of the Bering Strait.

She says she feels change begins with one person's vision. "That vision is shared, and the strength of that vision grows, and through that growth change begins."

"There are no borders in the ocean," she says, "just imaginary lines dividing countries. People might believe in those lines less if I swim across them."

Now Try This

Lynne Cox has swum in many places all around the world. See if you can trace her adventures and discover more about the difficulties she faced during each one.

Cape of Good Hope, South Africa, 1979

Prudhoe Bay, Alaska, 2007

Cook Strait, New Zealand, 1975

Lake Titicaca, South America, 1992

1. Use a world atlas to find the site of each of Lynne's swims shown here.

2. Use a library or the Internet to find out more about the waters in each place.

3. Write a brief summary about each of these places. Include facts about

- the temperature of the water
- the animals that live in the water
- the land on each side of the water
- any special dangers a swimmer might face

4. Share what you've learned with a classmate or relative.

Glossary

channel *n.* a narrow stretch of water that separates two areas of land

currents *n.* masses of water that flow in one direction

endurance *n.* the ability to keep going despite weakness or pain

fatigue *n.* extreme tiredness

hostile *adj.* acting or feeling angry or unfriendly

mainland *n.* the main part of country's land that doesn't include islands

pace *n.* the speed at which a person does something

pilot *n.* a person who guides a ship through a specific stretch of water